MG 6.1 1.0 pts

AMERICA'S SUPERNATURAL SECRETS™

GHOSTs in America

Diane Bailey

rosen publishing's
rosen
central

NEW YORK

Published in 2012 by The Rosen Publishing Group, Inc.
29 East 21st Street, New York, NY 10010

First Edition

Library of Congress Cataloging-in-Publication Data

Bailey, Diane, 1966–
Ghosts in America / Diane Bailey. — 1st ed.
    p. cm.
Includes bibliographical references (p.   ) and index.
ISBN 978-1-4488-5527-8 (library binding)—ISBN 978-1-4488-5572-8 (pbk.)—
ISBN 978-1-4488-5573-5 (6-pack)
1. Ghosts—United States. I. Title.
BF1472.U6B33 2012
133.10973—dc23

                                                                    2011017457

Manufactured in the United States of America

CPSIA Compliance Information: Batch #W12YA: For further information, contact Rosen Publishing, New York, New York, at 1-800-237-9932.

Contents

Introduction

Sshhhh! Did you hear that? That bump? That moan? That creaking door? Did you see something out of the corner of your eye—a floating figure, or a dark shadow, or maybe a glowing light? It can't be—there's no one there! Or is there?

If you believe in ghosts, you have a lot of company. Recently, the news organization the Associated Press conducted a poll. It found that one-third of Americans believe in ghosts. Almost 25 percent of people said they'd actually had a ghostly experience. Ghosts make many people nervous or scared, but sometimes they can be comforting, especially if it is the spirit of a departed friend or relative. Then, their presence reassures the living that they are OK.

People across the United States see ghosts every day—or at least they think they do. They haunt houses, hotels, battlefields, cemeteries, and roadways. Some spirits, instead of crossing over into the world of the dead, stick around because they have a job to do. It might be to comfort or warn a surviving family member about something. It might be to seek revenge on someone who harmed them when they were still living. Or it might be that they are just lonely and want to visit the people and places they knew in life.

Ghost stories were being told thousands of years ago, and they are still popular today. Some people are interested in learning why ghosts return to the world of the living. Others just like to be spooked by a super-natural story.

A family of ghosts takes up residence on a lawn in Massachusetts for Halloween. The popularity of ghost costumes and decorations shows how they have taken up residence in people's imaginations, too.

It's easy to get creeped out by strange sounds or weird visions. Of course, lots of them have perfectly normal explanations. It might just be a breeze that's fluttering the curtains or rattling the window. Sometimes it's hard to tell, especially if you're in the dark, alone…

Or not.

chapter 1

Graveyard Tales

ead men tell no tales. That's how the saying goes, but some talkative ghosts have plenty to say, especially when it's about someone who did them wrong. In some cases, their appearances have made the living do some digging—back into the grave—to find out what really happened.

A Suspicious Death

On a cold day in January, 1897, eleven-year-old Andy Jones entered the home of Edward and Zona Shue, a couple who lived in Greenbrier County, West Virginia. Edward had sent him there to find out if his wife needed anything from the store. But Andy did not get a shopping list from Zona. Instead, he saw her sprawled on the floor, dead.

When the local doctor, George Knapp, arrived at the couple's home to examine the body, a seemingly grief-stricken Edward was crying and hysterical. Knapp wasn't sure what had happened. He thought he saw bruises on Zona's neck. Nonetheless, he was anxious to get through the ordeal and pronounced Zona dead from natural causes.

Zona's mother, Mary Jane Heaster, was suspicious. Her daughter had been married to Edward for only a few months. Mary Jane had never liked

A historical marker relates the facts involved in the strange case of the Greenbrier Ghost of West Virginia. The story continues to fascinate people more than a century later.

him. She wondered whether there was more to the story. But first, she had to take care of the sad business of burying her daughter.

Zona's body was laid out for the wake, an event where people gather to say good-bye to the dead. During this time, Edward behaved strangely. He would not allow anyone to get too close to his dead wife. He carefully wrapped a scarf around her neck, and insisted on being the only one to arrange the pillows around her head. Still, people noticed that Zona's head seemed "loose."

One night in 1832, a Pennsylvania man walking home near a place called "Duffy's Cut" saw a strange sight: dancing ghosts. "They looked as if they were a kind of green and blue fire, and there they were hopping and bobbing on their graves," he reported. He believed the ghosts were Irish railroad workers who had died from cholera a few weeks before.

Then in 2000, Bill Watson was in the area and saw three mysterious, glowing figures. He became convinced he'd seen the same thing as the man in 1832, and decided to launch an investigation. Since then, researchers have detected significant paranormal activity at the site. In addition, scientists have examined the bodies. Instead of dying from cholera, evidence shows the men may have been murdered, probably to stop the disease from spreading. Perhaps their ghosts have been trying, for almost two hundred years, to set the record straight.

After the wake, Mary Jane removed the sheet that Zona had rested on in the coffin. It smelled bad, so she washed it. The water in the tub turned red! When she pulled the sheet out, it had turned pink. Mary Jane was convinced this was a sign. She believed the mysterious stains were blood, and that Zona had not died naturally. She had been murdered!

Mary Jane was convinced that Zona could tell her what had really happened. For the next few weeks, she prayed for her daughter to come to her and reveal the truth.

Then one night, the air in the room where Mary Jane slept grew cold. It was not just the chill of winter. It was the cold surrounding the visitor who had appeared—Zona's ghost. Over the course of four nights, Zona returned to her mother and woke her up. She told a terrible story. Zona confided that Edward had not been a good husband. He was often mean to her. On the day of her death, he had flown into a rage just because Zona did not have any meat to cook for his dinner. Then, he attacked her and broke her neck!

As Mary Jane listened in horror, Zona's ghost slowly swiveled her head completely around to prove what she was saying. No wonder Edward had not let anyone near Zona's body. If he had, someone might have discovered the true cause of her death. Mary Jane had the proof she needed. She went to the authorities.

The Case Is Reopened

Meanwhile, other facts about Edward were discovered. He was new to town, and people had not known him well. It turned out that Zona was his third wife.

The grave of Zona Heaster Shue remains undisturbed today, but in the months following her death, the young woman did not rest in peace until her family had uncovered the truth about her murder.

He had beaten his first wife, and his second died suddenly. Even if some people did not fully believe Mary Jane's ghost story, there was no doubt that Edward's character was questionable. And many had noticed his strange behavior after Zona died.

Zona's body was exhumed, or dug up, and examined more closely. Doctors discovered that she had indeed died after someone had choked her. Edward was charged with murder and went to trial. The defense attorney had Mary Jane tell her "ghost story," hoping it would show she was not a reliable witness. The attorney asked her to admit the visions had been dreams, but Mary Jane remained firm. "I am not going to say that; for I am not going to lie," she said. In the end, the jury convicted Edward, and he was sent to prison.

Mary Jane was the only person who saw Zona's ghost, and some think she made the story up to catch Edward for the crime she was sure he had committed. On the day of Zona's death, an article in the local newspaper told about a man in Australia who said he had seen the ghost of a man who showed that he had been murdered. Maybe Mary Jane decided to try the same thing, and believed that by inventing the ghost story, she would gain the sympathy of the other townspeople.

No one will ever know. For the twenty years after that Mary Jane lived, she stood by her story, and Zona became known as a ghost who helped solve her own murder.

Chapter 2

Room for One More

In 2010, the New York Knicks basketball team stayed overnight at a historic Oklahoma City hotel before their game against the Oklahoma City Thunder. They lost badly the next day, but some players had an excuse: they'd been spooked by ghosts at the hotel! There's something about hotels that ghosts seem to like. Maybe it's that they are always open for guests—even ghostly ones!

Where's the Party?

The sounds of clinking glasses and people talking fill the Brookdale Lodge, located in Santa Cruz, California. Big band music comes from the Fireside Room and the Pool Room. The jukebox in the Mermaid Room is playing. It sounds like fun. The only problem is that the rooms are empty—at least of living people.

Who are these ghostly diners? Maybe they are past guests, reliving the heyday of the Brookdale. From the 1920s through the 1940s, it was a popular resort with famous people, including President Herbert Hoover and movie stars such as Mae West. Songs were even written about the Brookdale, including "My Brookdale Hideway," "A Place Known as Brookdale," and "Beautiful Brookdale Lodge."

Is this hallway really deserted? In historic hotels, ghosts may lurk in the rooms or roam long corridors as they haunt unsuspecting visitors who thought they were alone!

One of Brookdale's big attractions was the dining room, called the Brookroom. It was built so that a stream, which came down from the surrounding mountains, ran right through the middle of it. Rocks, trees, and bushes added to the natural feel. Tables overlooked the rustic scene, which brought the majestic beauty of the surrounding redwood forests inside. For a child, it must have been a perfect spot to play—until tragedy struck.

Sarah Logan

Sometime in the 1940s, a six-year-old girl, Sarah Logan, drowned in the Brookroom creek. But it seems Sarah wasn't ready to leave her home at the

Brookdale. Employees and guests have spotted a little girl, dressed in a fancy, blue-and-white dress. She is playing by the fireplace or on the balcony above the dining area. Sometimes the little girl will approach guests, crying and upset, and ask them to help her find her mother. The guests are happy to help, but when they turn away to look for the missing woman, the little girl vanishes. Employees are convinced this little girl is Sarah. Perhaps it is even more frightening that the girl does not appear particularly "ghostly." She was "very clear, like a whole person," according to reports. That is, until the people watching her saw her ghost run through a solid wall!

As Sarah looks for her mother, her mother may also be looking for her. Diners in the Brookroom have reported seeing a woman floating above the creek, as if she was standing on a bridge that is no longer there. In addition, the smell of gardenias envelops the room at night—even though that particular

Battle Scars and Scares

As one of the United States' oldest cities, New Orleans, Louisiana, has seen much of America's bloody history. The Battle of New Orleans was fought there in 1815. During the Civil War, the city sent thousands of men to fight for the Confederate cause. The soldiers from both wars are now all dead—but not necessarily gone.

One building at the Hotel Provincial served as a military hospital during both wars. Guests have reported hearing the groans of wounded soldiers and seeing their bloodied bodies. Sometimes guests have experienced soldiers reaching out to them for help. Bloodstains sometimes appear—and then vanish—from the sheets. One worker reported that when riding an elevator, the doors opened and he saw an entire hospital ward filled with patients and nurses. Perhaps these soldiers do not realize that the war is over, and they will flower isn't planted anywhere in the Brookdale. Psychics called in to investigate the Brookdale's hauntings think the woman could be Sarah's mother.

Spirits from the Past

Sarah's death seemed to change the fates and fortunes of the Brookdale. The music faded, and throughout the 1940s and 1950s, disreputable characters like gangsters started to fill the Brookdale's rooms. They may have even filled

The Brookdale Lodge has changed drastically over the decades, but through it all, psychic investigators have continued to search for and identify the many

other places at the Brookdale—underneath it. Rumors spread that bodies were buried in the secret rooms and passageways that had been built below the lodge. It's said there is a haunted meat locker, now sealed off. There, mobsters murdered their victims because their screams would not be heard through the thick walls.

Room 46 seems particularly haunted. An employee who lived in it reported that she would see objects flying across the room at night. Once she felt someone even sit down next to her and touch her. She also saw several people, such as ballroom dancers who seemed to be enjoying a night of entertainment. There were also more sobering apparitions, like a man with his face badly cut, and another with his eye falling out of its socket. Perhaps these were victims from the Brookdale's seedy period as a gangster hangout.

One spirit has been identified as a lumberjack named George, who could be from the lodge's early days as a lumber mill in the late 1800s. He can be heard in the conference room, where doors slam for no reason. Sometimes he is met behind the lodge, in a spot where wood was chopped to feed the fireplaces.

Something about the Brookdale seems to attract—or even trap—ghosts. Over the years, the hotel's owners have called in psychics to investigate the ghosts. They have identified forty-nine different spirits! The Brookdale seems to turn no one away—especially those who have no other place on earth to go.

chapter 3

Can't Stay Still

Some ghosts are quiet and shy. If you blink, you might miss them. But others are definitely more outgoing. They are attention-seekers who refuse to be ignored. The word *poltergeist* is German for "noisy ghost." Certainly, these ghosts make themselves heard!

A Screwy Situation

It was just an ordinary day in early February 1958 when Lucille Herrmann, thirteen, and her brother James, twelve, came home from school to their house on Long Island, New York. But within minutes, things got weird. For no reason, the tops started popping off the bottles all over the house! Bleach in the basement and starch in the kitchen. Shampoo and medicine in the bathroom. A bottle of holy water in the master bedroom. The Herrmann children and their mother were mystified. When Mr. Herrmann got home from work that evening, he had no explanation either. All the bottles had screw-tops. They could not just fall off.

At first the family believed the strange incident was just a one-time thing. They decided not to worry about it too much. But then, a few days later, it happened again. Now Mr. Herrmann was suspicious. James was good at science. Mr. Herrmann suspected he might be pulling an elaborate prank. More bottles exploded a few days later. Some of them even moved, by themselves, as he watched. Mr. Herrmann accused James of playing a trick, but

As a poltergiest terrorized a Long Island family, psychologist J. Gaither Pratt was called in to investigate. Here he talks with James Herrmann, who many believed was subconsciously causing the disturbance.

James denied it. After investigating, he became convinced his son was innocent. Maybe there was a logical explanation, but the Herrmanns could not find it. It seemed the house was being bothered by a ghost—and a very rambunctious one, at that.

Looking for Answers

Mr. Herrmann decided to call in outside help. He started with the police. They were skeptical at first, but the detective on the case, Joseph Tozzi, decided the Herrmanns had a real problem when he witnessed the strange activity himself. However, he had no idea what was causing the disturbances. Next the Herrmanns called in a priest to bless the house. This did not help either.

Meanwhile, the poltergeist, who had been nicknamed "Popper," was branching out from bottles. Figurines and dishes were lifted from their resting places and hovered in the air. Then, the poltergeist began hurling objects several feet across the room. The items got bigger: while James was doing his homework one evening, his record player flew across the room. A globe zoomed down the hallway, almost hitting Detective Tozzi, who was in the house at the time. A bookcase fell over.

The incidents captured the attention of the media. Newspaper and television reporters showed up to find out what was going on. People from all over the country wrote to the Herrmanns, suggesting explanations and solutions. One thought it must be Martians. Another decided it was the Russians, tunneling under Long Island in order to attack New York. Still another suggested it was the spirit of a dead Indian chief.

Many natural causes were investigated as well. Detective Tozzi ruled out underground streams causing a strange magnetic field; radio waves; sonic booms from nearby aircraft; changes in the underground water level; and a downdraft from the fireplace. By now, the Herrmanns were ready for anyone's help. That's when scientists from Duke University, who specialized in parapsychology, decided to take a look.

A Psychological Basis?

Dr. J. Gaither Pratt and Dr. William Roll had been studying cases in which people could move objects without actually touching them. This is called psychokinesis, or PK. Because poltergeist activity often occurs around teenage children, some scientists think it has to do with the children's growing energies, which they are unable to express otherwise. Without necessarily meaning to, the children apply their energy to the objects around them, making them move.

Some people have the power to manipulate objects with the force of their minds, an ability called psychokinesis. Here a magician bends a metal spoon as part of his act.

The doctors wondered if this might be the case at the Herrmanns' house. Most of the incidents had occurred when James was in the room or nearby. One night, when the family spent a night away from home and left the house with Detective Tozzi, nothing happened. Psychologists did determine that James had some hostility toward his parents. Even if James was somehow causing the activity, however, the paranormal researchers did not believe he was doing it on purpose. Pratt told a reporter, "The family was much too shaken for it to be a colossal hoax."

A Troubled Employee

Drs. Pratt and Roll worked on another poltergeist case a few years later. A nineteen-year-old man named Julio was working at a warehouse for a company in Miami, Florida. Soon after he started his job, odd things began happening. Boxes moved when no one was near them. Items fell off shelves and broke. The company manager finally called in the police, and then Pratt and Roll got involved. They noticed that most of the activity happened when Julio was around. They thought he might be using psychokinesis. Indeed, Julio was a troubled young man, upset with his family and his boss. He actually liked it when things got broken, he said, but added that he had not actually done it. However, the doctors gave Julio several psychological tests. These showed that he did have some psychokinetic powers. And when he no longer worked at the warehouse, the incidents stopped.

On March 10, a little more than a month after the poltergeist arrived, it left. It popped the top off one last bleach bottle as its final good-bye. No one—from plumbers to police to paranormal psychologists—ever figured out for sure what caused the poltergeist activity. The Herrmanns were just glad that whoever it was had decided not to "pop in" anymore!

Chapter 4

Unfinished Business

You've probably gone to school and forgotten your homework before. But what if you never had another chance to get it? It seems some ghosts come back to reclaim important items that they've left behind.

Firing at a Ghost

In 1916, when Robert Lamont moved into a place called Summerwind, in northern Wisconsin, he had big plans. He converted the former fishing lodge into a mansion for his family. They lived there for several years. But then, one evening when Lamont was eating in the kitchen, the door leading to the basement began to shake. Suddenly it opened, and Lamont saw a man standing there. According to some accounts, the man even tried to attack Lamont.

Lamont pulled out his pistol and fired two quick shots. Perhaps Lamont did not realize at first who—or what—his opponent really was: a ghost. But he soon found out because guns don't work on ghosts. The figure was not killed, or even wounded. In fact, he wasn't there at all. Only the bullet holes in the door remained. Convinced that his house was haunted, Lamont moved out soon after.

For the next few decades, things were quiet at Summerwind, if not exactly happy. Several different people owned the house, but it cost too much money to keep up. Besides, the house gave them a creepy feeling. One by one, they gave up.

The stark and decaying Summerwind Mansion looks forbidding in its place atop a northern Wisconsin hill. The mansion was so haunted that it drove entire families out.

Then, in the early 1970s, Arnold and Ginger Hinshaw moved in with their children. If ghosts had been sleeping at Summerwind, the Hinshaws woke them up. The paranormal activity began almost immediately. Voices belonging to no one came from empty rooms. Shadows from people who weren't there crept down the hallways. Windows and doors would be found open when they had been left closed. Several times, the family saw a floating apparition of a woman. Nonetheless, they decided to try to live with the ghosts.

But the hauntings took their toll on the Hinshaws. Arnold's behavior turned bizarre. He began playing the organ in a frenzy, crashing down on the keys

Grandma's Ring

The parents of a four-year-old Massachusetts girl were worried when their daughter said she had been talking to the ghost of her dead grandmother. And yet, they were not sure she was making it up. Some of the things the girl said were things only her grandmother could have known. But why was the ghost there? What did she want? A ghost-hunting team came to investigate. They picked up signs of paranormal activity, such as cold temperatures in the room. Then, the little girl began having a conversation with the ghost. After a few minutes, as if following instructions, she went to the basement and began looking through boxes. She opened one and pulled out a diamond ring. "Grandma wants her ring," she told her parents. The next day, the family visited the grandmother's grave and buried her ring next to her. Afterward, the paranormal experiences stopped.

and frightening the rest of the family. He had a nervous breakdown, and Ginger tried to commit suicide. Eventually, Arthur had to seek treatment for his mental problems, while Ginger and the children moved in with her parents. No doubt the strange happenings at Summerwind contributed to the Hinshaws' problems. But Ginger had not told her parents what had happened, and her father decided to convert the house into a hotel and restaurant. When Ginger found out, her father later wrote, she was horrified and warned him against it. She told him, "There is a presence there. Something powerful and evil."

A Good Story Indeed

Nonetheless, Ginger's father, Raymond Bober, decided to move forward with his plans and began renovating Summerwind. As Ginger had feared, the

Encounters with ghosts, like the one portrayed in this cleverly manip-
ulated image, terrorized residents of Summerwind Mansion. Some
heard strange noises or saw shadows, while others claimed to have
actually interacted with the ghosts.

ghosts came back. Raymond's wife, Marie, felt unsettled by the house. She felt as if someone was watching her. Raymond's son, Karl, also reported having strange experiences when he was alone at the house.

As work on the house started, the weird activity continued. The workmen's tools disappeared. They reported feeling uneasy in the house. Many of them refused to come to work. Even creepier was the fact that the house seemed to grow and shrink. Raymond would measure rooms and then find the next day that they were an entirely different size. Even photographs taken only a few minutes apart showed different dimensions.

What was going on?

Raymond claimed he had the answer. He said he had been visited in a dream by the ghost of Jonathan Carver. Carver was an eighteenth-century explorer who traveled with Sioux Indians and later wrote a book about his experiences. The editor for his book, along with some of Carver's heirs, later said that Carver had received a land deed, signed by the Sioux Indian chiefs. This deed would have given him a large amount of land in Wisconsin. No one could prove the story, however.

Nonetheless, Raymond said that Carver told him the land deed was buried in the foundation of Summerwind. Raymond concluded the house's hauntings were a result of Carver looking for his property—and trying to scare off anyone who got in his way. Of course, no one could ever prove this story either. Despite looking, no one ever found a deed in the foundation. Skeptics think Raymond invented the Carver ghost story to increase business at his future resort.

However, his plans were never finished, and Summerwind was left to languish. Then, in 1988, lightning struck the house and it burned to the ground. If Summerwind's ghosts—whoever they were—just wanted to keep people away, they got their wish. Today, nothing remains of Summerwind but the chimney, the foundation, and the stories.

Chapter 5

On the Move

"Stay active!" If that is good advice in life, then why not in death? Some ghosts are not content to just rattle around the house or have a comfortable, fireside haunt. Instead, they are always on the move.

In Texas, a man named Brit Bailey insisted that he wanted to be buried standing up. After all, he said, he had spent his life roaming the Texas range. He did not plan to stop just because he was dead. True to his prediction, his ghost was seen on the prairie for years to come. Maybe these ghosts are restless. Or maybe they are just a little homesick, reluctant to leave their old stomping grounds.

A Reckless Ride

Settlers heading west on the Oregon Trail, exhausted from weeks of hard travel, surely would have welcomed the sight of the Fort Laramie trading post in Wyoming. Fort Laramie was established in 1834 as a fur trading post. Later it became an important stronghold for the U.S. military during the Indian wars of the nineteenth century. The fort was located in the middle of hard, dangerous country. In those days, people would have said it was no place for a woman.

But not all women agreed. When Fort Laramie was part of the American Fur Company, the agent in charge brought his daughter to live with him. She

In the mid-1800s, Fort Laramie, Wyoming, was frequented by cowboys and travelers on their way west. The harsh living conditions and threat of Indian attacks made it a dangerous place to live.

was a sophisticated city girl, educated in high-class schools on the East Coast. She was also a skilled horsewoman. She loved to take her favorite black horse on long rides around the grounds of the trading post.

Her father, however, worried about her safety. He instructed the men who worked for him to watch over her. And he warned her not to leave the post without an escort. Beyond the boundaries of the post were all kinds of dangers. There were hostile Indians, for one. And there was the unforgiving landscape of Wyoming, where the vast stretches of Great Plains to the east came up against the imposing Rocky Mountains.

When a cholera epidemic struck the military post of Fort Hays, Kansas, in 1867, Elizabeth Polly tended to the dying soldiers. It was exhausting work, so Polly would sometimes take a walk on nearby Sentinel Hill to relax. Then, tragically, she got the disease. She wanted to be buried at the top of the hill, but it was too rocky to dig her grave. She was buried at the base instead.

But Polly's ghost did not stay put. Over the years, several people have reported seeing a mysterious blue light on the hill that is believed to be her. Others have seen a woman in a blue dress. In 1950, a police officer reported that he had hit a woman matching this description with his car, but there was no body. Some think that Polly's ghost wanted to return to the place she loved in life—the summit of Sentinel Hill.

Perhaps the girl was headstrong, determined to rebel against her father. Or perhaps she simply longed for the freedom of riding in the open hills. Either way, she defied his orders to stay close to home. One day, when he was away on business, she left the post. Her father's men chased after her, but she eluded them—forever.

Hours passed, then days. When the girl did not return, her father searched for her, hoping to find answers. Had she been captured or murdered by Indians? Killed in a bad fall? Become hopelessly lost and starved to death? No one would ever know. The girl was never seen again—at least not alive.

The "Lady in Green" Returns

About twenty years after the girl disappeared, James Allison, a lieutenant with the U.S. military, reported for duty at Fort Laramie. One afternoon, when he

A statue of Elizabeth Polly memorializes the frontier woman's tireless efforts to help soldiers sick with cholera. Her ghost is believed to still roam the area in Kansas where she lived her last days.

was out hunting, he became separated from the rest of his group. He called out, but no one answered. Then he was surprised to see a horse galloping toward him. The rider was not one of the men from his hunting party. Instead, it was a woman on a black mount, dressed in a striking green riding habit. As she rode past him, she touched a jeweled quirt, or riding whip, to the horse's flank.

Lieutenant Allison chased the mysterious woman, but he could not catch her. When he came over a small rise, he saw that she and her horse had vanished. Shaken, Lieutenant Allison saw that the pair had left no tracks in the dust. He realized that he had not heard any hoof beats either. His dog also seemed upset, perhaps sensing a ghostly presence as well. That evening, back at the post, he told his commanding officer what he had seen. The officer was not surprised. He confirmed, "You have seen our Lady in Green. She appears near the fort about every seven years, and she means no harm."

Lieutenant Allison's curiosity was sparked. He began to ask around to find out more. He spoke to an Indian woman who lived near the fort. She reported that she had seen the girl leave on her "fatal ride," and described the girl's clothing just as Lieutenant Allison had seen it. The woman also confirmed that other Indians and trappers in the area had seen her. Years later, he heard some cowboys talking about seeing the ghostly horse and rider. Reported sightings continued late into the twentieth century as the Lady in Green got what she always wanted—the chance to ride free.

Chapter 6

Ghosts in Popular Culture

G host stories have been around for as long as people have been alive...and dead. Today, ghosts show up not only in attics and around campfires, but on television and in the movies. It's not always clear what's real and what's entertainment, but one thing is sure: people love to hear about ghosts.

The Spiritualist Movement

Although ghosts are nothing new, they have not always been as accepted in society as they are today. People might believe in ghosts, or they might not believe, but either way they did not go around discussing ghosts in polite company. That began to change around the 1850s. A philosophy called spiritualism began to take hold. Its followers believed people could communicate with the dead, and they actively tried to do so.

Mediums are people who are skilled in summoning and communicating with spirits (or at least say they can). Thousands of mediums went into business in the United States in the 1800s. Some wanted to help people talk to ghosts. Some probably just wanted to cash in on the "spirit boom."

Certainly, many mediums were fakes. Leah, Margaret, and Kate Fox were three sisters who lived in New York. They claimed to be able to communicate with ghosts, and many people sought out their services. They had

Mysterious faces surrounded in mist were artificially inserted into this family photograph from the early twentieth century. Family members wanting evidence of lost loved ones frequently believed such deceptions.

successful careers as mediums for many years before confessing that their talents were just an act.

Despite the acts of fraud, the New England Spiritualist Association estimated that there were two million believers in the United States. In 1854, a senator from Illinois presented a petition to Congress asking the government to "investigate communications from the dead." Not everyone was tolerant of the movement. In Alabama, a law was passed to stop people from making a public display of being a medium. Nonetheless, the spiritualism movement in America was strong until about the 1920s, when it finally began to fade.

Ghosts in Books, Movies, and TV

Next time you are tempted to complain about your parents, think of the alternative: would you like to be raised in a graveyard by ghosts? That's exactly what happens in The Graveyard Book, by Neil Gaiman. However, the arrangement works out well for the main character, Nobody Owens. His foster parents teach him some handy ghostly tricks that help him defeat his enemies.

Ghosts show up (and fade away) in plenty of other children's books, too. In J. K. Rowling's Harry Potter series, ghosts wander down the halls and through the walls at Hogwarts. Each house at Hogwarts even has its own ghost mascot. Rowling does not make her ghosts particularly mysterious or scary. Instead, they are treated like regular characters who just happen to be dead.

Many popular movies have also featured ghosts. The 1990 movie Ghost features a man who returns to warn his girlfriend that she is in danger. In this film, the ghost character is not scary at all—he is a hero. In the 1999 movie The Sixth Sense, a young boy is frightened by the ghosts he sees. However, he is encouraged to talk to them, and eventually he realizes that they are simply spirits who need help settling their business in life before they

Author Neil Gaiman reads from his novel *The Graveyard Book* during a 2008 appearance. The award-winning children's book features a main character who interacts with several ghostly characters.

can move on. In the 1980s, *Poltergeist* movies came out. These were more scary, as the ghosts involved had some sinister motivations. Several recent horror movies have gone for "chills and thrills," featuring ghosts who are clearly out to terrorize their victims.

Ghosts have floated onto the small screen as well. Popular series like *Medium* and *Ghost Whisperer* feature characters who interact with ghosts on a regular basis. In *Medium*, the series' main character is a medium and psychic who helps local law enforcement solve crimes based on her sightings. The main character in *Ghost Whisperer* is a little more reluctant. Despite

Ghost Tours

Lots of people claim to live in haunted houses. But for those who don't, there are plenty of opportunities to hear about—and maybe experience—ghosts. In cities across the United States, tourism companies offer "ghost tours" to visitors. During these, they report on hauntings and tell the stories of local ghosts. And even if you don't see a ghost, you can still get a T-shirt!

trying to live a normal life, she is constantly visited by ghosts and must figure out how to help them.

Reveal Yourself!

In 1984, the successful movie *Ghostbusters* told the story of three men who started a business hunting down ghosts. The movie was a comedy, but many real-life ghost hunters take their jobs more seriously. Across the United States, there are dozens of organizations devoted to investigating paranormal activity. Unlike the mediums of a century ago, however, these people do not rely on candlelight and a creepy atmosphere. Instead, they are equipped with scientific instruments that can pick up actual physical changes in the environment, such as electromagnetic fields or cold spots in the atmosphere. These can indicate the presence of ghosts.

The Atlantic Paranormal Society (TAPS) is a team of paranormal investigators who look into stories of ghosts and hauntings. Their adventures are filmed and gathered into a TV show, *Ghost Hunters*. Other shows like *Paranormal State* and *Psychic Kids: Paranormal Children* have similar premises. These shows are supposed to be based in reality. However, they regularly draw criticism for using questionable scientific methods or for outright inventing

Grant Wilson and Jason Hawes star in the television show *Ghost Hunters*. The paranormal investigators travel across the United States looking into reports of ghostly activity.

some of the stories. In addition, some think the sensational aspect of television makes studying the paranormal seem silly.

Still, there are many people who devote their time and skills to studying supernatural phenomena. They try to understand not only why the ghosts are there, but how some people can see them and even communicate with them. Perhaps ghost hunting television shows are only a fad. But ghost stories themselves will not go away. After all, most people do not go out hunting ghosts—it's the ghosts who find them!

Glossary

apparition The appearance of a ghost.

cholera A highly contagious disease that causes dehydration and often death.

disreputable Having a bad reputation or character.

elude To deliberately escape from someone.

exhumed To remove a body from a grave after burial.

fraud A deceitful action or person.

heir A person who inherits money or property from someone who dies.

heyday The period of time when something is at its best or most popular.

languish To become inactive or unused.

ordeal A difficult or trying situation.

paranormal Something that is outside the realm of normality and cannot be explained through science.

parapsychology The study of mental phenomena that cannot be explained through science.

petition A formal request for action, signed by multiple people.

poltergeist A type of ghost that moves objects and makes a lot of noise.

psychokinesis The power to move objects using the mind.

quirt A riding whip.

rambunctious Extremely active; rowdy.

rustic Having an earthy, natural feel.

supernatural Something that cannot be explained by natural phenomena.

tolerant Willing to accept attitudes that are different.

American Society for Psychical Research, Inc. (ASPR)
5 West 73rd Street
New York, NY 10023
(212) 799-5050
E-mail: aspr@aspr.com
Web site: http://www.aspr.com
Founded in 1885, ASPR researches paranormal claims and activity and
     seeks to understand how they relate to issues of consciousness and
     existence.

The Atlantic Paranormal Society
2362 West Shore Road
Warwick, RI 02889
E-mail: help@the-atlantic-paranormal-society.com
Web site: http://www.the-atlantic-paranormal-society.com
Investigators at TAPS travel all over the United States looking into
     reported ghosts and hauntings. The team also has a television show,
     Ghost Hunters.

Committee for Skeptical Inquiry (CSI)
Box 703
Amherst, NY 14226
(716) 636-1425
E-mail: info@csicop.org
Web site: http://www.csicop.org
CSI strives to provide objective investigations of claims of paranormal activity
     using science, reason, and critical thinking.

Ghost Research Society
P.O. Box 205
Oak Lawn, IL 60454-0205
(708) 425-5163
Web site: http://www.ghostresearch.org
A team of researchers at the organization investigates reports of ghosts,
    hauntings, and poltergeists.'

Paranormal Research Society (PRS)
P.O. Box 403
State College, PA 16801
E-mail: society@paranormalresearchsociety.org
Web site: http://www.paranormalresearchsociety.org
PRS investigates paranormal phenomena from both a spiritual and sci-
    entific perspective, by studying parapsychology and conducting
    fieldwork.

Parapsychology Foundation
P.O. Box 1562
New York, NY 10021
(212) 628-1550
E-mail: office@parapsychology.org
Web site: http://www.parapsychology.org
The foundation forwards the study of psychic phenomena by providing infor-
    mation and resources to scientists, scholars, and the general public.

Society of Paranormal Enounters of Canada, Training and Entity Research
    (S.P.E.C.T.E.R.)
77 Speedvale Avenue West, Apt. C
Guelph, ON
N1H 1K1
Canada

Web site: http://specterweb.tripod.com/guelph
A team of investigators provides home evaluations, trying to determine the cause of paranormal activity and helping people to understand what can be done.

Web Sites

Due to the changing nature of Internet links, Rosen Publishing has developed an online list of Web sites related to the subject of this book. This site is updated regularly. Please use this link to access the list:

http://www.rosenlinks.com/amss/ghos

For Further Reading

Abbott, Tony. *The Haunting of Derek Stone*. New York, NY: Scholastic, 2009.

Belanger, Jeff. *Who's haunting the White House?: The President's Mansion and the Ghosts Who Live There*. New York, NY: Sterling Publishing, 2008.

Brucken, Kelli M. *Ghosts*. Farmington Hills, MI: Kidhaven Press, 2006.

DeFelice, Cynthia. *The Ghost of Poplar Point*. New York, NY: Farrar, Straus and Giroux, 2007.

Duffield, Katy. *Poltergeists*. Farmington Hills, MI: Kidhaven Press, 2007.

Ellis, Melissa Martin. *The Everything Ghost Hunting Book*. Avon, MA: Adams Media, 2009.

Gaiman, Neil. *The Graveyard Book*. New York, NY: HarperCollins, 2008.

Gee, Joshua. *Encyclopedia Horrifica: The Terrifying TRUTH! About Vampires, Ghosts, Monsters, and More*. New York, NY: Scholastic, 2007.

Gibson, Marley, Patrick Burns, and Dave Schrader. *The Other Side: A Teen's Guide to Ghost Hunting and the Paranormal*. Boston, MA: Houghton Mifflin Harcourt, 2009.

Gudgeon, Chris. *Ghost Trackers: The Unreal World of Ghosts, Ghost-Hunting, and the Paranormal*. Toronto, Ontario: Tundra Books, 2010.

Hawes, Jason, and Grant Wilson. *Ghost Hunt: Chilling Tales of the Unknown*. New York, NY: Little, Brown and Company, 2010.

Krensky, Stephen. *Ghosts*. Minneapolis, MN: Lerner Publications, 2008.

Lace, William W. *Ghost Hunters*. San Diego, CA: Reference Point Press, 2010.

Marcovitz, Hal. *Poltergeists*. San Diego, CA: Reference Point Press, 2010.

Osborne, Mary Pope, and Natalie Pope Boyce. *Ghosts: A Nonfiction Companion to A Good Night for Ghosts*. New York, NY: Random House, 2009.

Oxlade, Chris. *The Mystery of Haunted Houses*. Chicago, IL: Heinemann Library, 2006.

Ruby, Lois. *The Secret of Laurel Oaks*. New York, NY: Tom Doherty Associates, 2008.

Stefoff, Rebecca. *Ghosts and Spirits*. Tarrytown, NY: Marshall Cavendish Benchmark, 2008.

Stewart, Gail B. *Ghosts*. San Diego, CA: Reference Point Press, 2010.

Stewart, Gail B. *Hauntings*. San Diego, CA: Reference Point Press, 2010.

Bibliography

Birnes, William J., and Joel Martin. *The Haunting of America: From the Salem Witch Trials to Harry Houdini*. New York, NY: Tom Doherty Associates, 2009.

HauntedAmericaTours.com. "Top Ten Haunted Hotels in the United States of America." Retrieved January 31, 2011 (http://www.hauntedamericatours.com/toptenhaunted/toptenhauntedhotels).

Hawes, Jason, Grant Wilson, and Michael Jan Friedman. *Ghost Hunting: True Stories of Unexplained Phenomena from The Atlantic Paranormal Society*. New York, NY: Simon & Schuster, 2007.

LegendsofAmerica.com. "Kansas Legends: Fort Hays—History & Hauntings." Retrieved January 28, 2011 (http://www.legendsofamerica.com/ks-forthays.html).

Lyle, Katie Letcher. *The Man Who Wanted Seven Wives*. Chapel Hill, NC: Algonquin Books, 1986.

MontereyBay.org. "Brookdale Lodge: Haunted or Not?" Retrieved January 28, 2011 (http://montereybay.org/haunted-ghost-brookdale-lodge.html)

Norman, Michael, and Beth Scott. *Historic Haunted America*. New York, NY: Tom Doherty Associates, 2007.

Rotondaro, Vinnie. "Why Real-life Ghost Hunters Hate 'Ghost Hunters.'" Salon.com, October 30, 2010. Retrieved January 30, 2011 (http://webcache.googleusercontent.com/search?q=cache:VvY4kbmQmqoJ:www.salon.com/entertainment/tv/2010/10/30/ghost_hunters).

Sceurman, Mark, and Mark Moran. *Weird Hauntings*. New York, NY: Sterling Publishing, 2006.

Stefko, Jill. "Greenbrier West Virginia Phantom Zona Heaster." Suite101.com. Retrieved January 26, 2011 (http://www.suite101.com/content/greenbrier-west-virginia-phantom-a20786).

Stefko, Jill. "Miami, Florida Poltergeist." Suite101.com. Retrieved January 31, 2011 (http://www.suite101.com/content/ miami-florida-poltergeist-a24100).

Steiger, Brad. *Real Ghosts, Restless Spirits, and Haunted Places.* Canton, MI: Visible Ink Press, 2003.

Taylor, Troy. "Popper the Poltergeist: Strange Happenings on New York's Long Island." PrairieGhosts.com. Retrieved January 24, 2011 (http:// www.prairieghosts.com/popper.html).

Taylor, Troy. "Summerwind: Wisconsin's Most Haunted House." PrairieGhosts.com. Retrieved January 28, 2011 (http://www.prairieg- hosts.com/summer.html).

Valania, Jonathan. "Murder in the Time of Cholera." PhiladelphiaWeekly. com. Retrieved January 28, 2011 (http://www.philadelphiaweekly. com/news-and-opinion/Murder-in-the-Time-of-Cholera.html).

Von Bober, Wolffgang. *The Carver Effect.* Harrisburg, PA: Stackpole Books, 1979.

Index

About the Author

The house Diane Bailey grew up in wasn't terribly haunted, but occasionally ghosts would stop by to remind the family that they weren't alone. Bailey now lives in an un-haunted house in Kansas with two sons and two dogs. She has written more than twenty books on a variety of nonfiction topics.

Photo Credits